The Dream Realm

Unlock, Interpret, & Govern Your Dreams

D'Andrea Bolden

Unless otherwise indicated, all scriptural quotations are from the *King James Version* of the Bible.

The Dream Realm: Unlock, Interpret & Govern Your Dreams

Published by:
Bolden Publishing
P.O. Box 2025
Kalamazoo, MI 49003
boldenenterprisesllc@gmail.com

Reproduction of text in whole or in part without the written consent by the author is not permitted and is unlawful according to the 1976 United States Copyright Act.

Copyright © 2018 by D'Andrea Bolden

All Rights Reserved

Library of Congress of Cataloging-in Publication Data:

An application to register this book for cataloging has been submitted to the Library of Congress

First Edition

Printed in the United States of America

D'Andrea Bolden

Table of Contents

UNLOCK YOUR DREAMS – Part 1

Introduction: p.3

The Dream Realm – Chapter 1: p.5

God's Language – Chapter 2: p.8

Purpose of Dreams – Chapter 3: p.11

Types of Dreams – Chapter 4: p.21

INTERPRET YOUR DREAMS – Part 2

Prophetic Symbols – Chapter 5: p.31

Dream Interpretation – Chapter 6: p.38

Dream Scope – Chapter 7: p.53

Dreams and Journals – Chapter 8: p.56

THE DREAM REALM – Part 3

Dreams + Creatives – Chapter 9 p.61

Dreams + Sensory Impairment – Chapter 10: p.67

Dreams + Children – Chapter 11: p.72

Dreams + Mental Health – Chapter 12: p.76

GOVERN YOUR DREAMS – Part 4

Governing Your Dream Realm – Chapter 14: p.80

Dreams + Warfare – Chapter 13: p.87

PART 1
UNLOCK YOUR DREAMS

Introduction

Do you have dreams from God? Do you understand the purpose of your dreams? Can you discern the source of your dreams? Are you always confused about the meaning of your dreams? Do you know how to govern and respond to your dreams?

If you answered yes to any of the questions above, then this is a book you should read. I know you are thinking, "it's just another book on dreams," but this is more than a book about dreams and interpretation.

The purpose of this book is to show, biblically, how God speaks to people through dreams and to make the reader more aware of how God speaks to them in dreams. This is a book to help readers begin to understand more about dreams and the purpose for them in their lives. This is not a book that will list a bunch of prophetic symbols and their meanings. The reason being is, after people look up various symbols and their meanings, many times they cannot find a definition that makes sense for their dreams. Dreams are not one size fits all and neither is the interpretation of those dreams. This book also shows the reader how to govern and respond to their dreams. We can no longer dream and get interpretations and pat ourselves on the back; but we must learn to move in the dream realm and respond to what God is saying. Dreams are so powerful, and they can yield strong messages, ideas, or even divine strategies.

Realm
/relm /
(noun) 1. An area or sphere, as of knowledge or activity:

Ref: Dictionary.com

The Dream Realm-1

Dream: a series of thoughts, images, or emotions occurring during sleep

Ref: Oxford Dictionaries Online

A lot of people have dreams; however, the majority do not understand these occurrences that happen while they are asleep. When we are asleep, that is the easiest time for us to dream because we are not busy, or able to be distracted as we are in a state of rest. When you are asleep, there are changes to your brain waves, temperature, heart rate, and even your breathing. While you are sleep, you go through a stage of the sleep cycle referred to as REM (rapid eye movement) and this is the time you are more prone to have dreams.

I cannot tell you how many people say that they have awakened from a dream in a state of complete bewilderment. The things that they saw and experienced in their dreams left them in a state of complete uncertainty. Most of the time, this is because the person having the dream had no understanding of what they saw in their dream.

Dreams are powerful, but many times, they are minimized or misunderstood. The Bible is filled with scriptures about dreams. Ironically, this is a topic that is not well understood or even addressed amongst believers. Sadly, the secular world, and even pagans, are more interested in dreams than the Christian church.

There has been so much negative and false information spewed in reference to dreams that some believers are afraid to dream or feel it's necessary to ignore or dismiss anything that they are seeing in dreams. With examples of dreams from the beginning to the end of the Bible, it is shocking to see how many believers quickly dismiss dreams, or only see them as demonic activity.

The lack of accurate and relevant information on the topic of dreams is alarming. The realm of dreams simply refers to the spiritual activity we experience that can be attributed to dreams. The reality is that most people can and do dream, regardless of frequency. More importantly, God can, and does, speak to His people through dreams!

Highlights

- Dreams occur while we are sleeping

- Dreams are not very well understood in the Christian church

- God can speak to His people through dreams

Dream
/drēm/
(noun) 1. A series of thoughts, images, and sensations occurring in a person's mind during sleep.

Ref: Oxford Dictionaries Online

Dreams: The Language of God-2

Language: the method of human communication, either spoken or written, consisting of the use of words in a structured and conventional way:

Ref: Oxford Dictionaries Online

If you are reading this book, you are fluent in the language we refer to as English. The English language is made up of letters that make sounds. These letters are used to make words and words are used to make statements. This is what we use in order to express ourselves and communicate one to another. We must remember that English, Spanish, Swahili, Braille, ASL and even German, are languages for humans to communicate and interact, but the language of God precedes all other languages, and it is superior to man's methods of communication.

People typically speak through reading, writing, or even signs which are understood by natural means, but God will speak to our spirit. Because natural methods are the ways that we are most comfortable receiving communication, God will speak to us in a still small voice, through His servants, and even through His written Word. On the other hand, however, dreams and visions are a bit different because God can speak to our spirit and bypass our natural processes and understanding. Have you had a dream where you did not hear one word, but you still knew exactly what was going on? This is because God was speaking to your spirit man.

Earthly language is for us and God does not need it to communicate. Dreams are a major component to understanding the language of God. Dreams typically combine visual, auditory, and tactile components to express a message to the person having the dream.

If the language of God was not different from other languages, people would not be perplexed by the dreams and visions that they see, but just like Pharaoh and King Nebuchadnezzar, many do not recognize or even understand the way God speaks. When a message has been communicated in a language that you do not understand, you will need to have the message translated. Translation allows a message to be converted from one language to another. Dream interpretation is the equivalent of translating a message from one language to another so that it can be understood. Because dreams and visions are a part of God's language and way of communication, the interpretation and understanding also comes from God.

Highlights

- Dreams are a part of God's language

- God can speak directly to our spirit

- Dreams and interpretation are mentioned in the Bible

- Many times, dreams require interpretation so that we can understand what God has spoken to us.

Language
/ˈlaNGgwij/

(noun) 1. the method of human communication, either spoken or written, consisting of the use of words in a structured and conventional way.

Ref: Oxford Dictionaries Online

Purpose of Dreams-3

I am hoping that after reading the first two chapters, you have a better understanding of what a dream is, because now, we are going to look at the purpose of dreams. God speaks to mankind in dreams for quite a few reasons.

A lot of people recognize that they are dreaming but may fail to attribute the dream to God. Some people do not believe that God speaks anymore, and some believe that dreams are always demonic. Then, there are others that fail to realize that God is using their dreams as a method to speak to them.

> **Job 33:14-16:** "Indeed God speaks once, Or twice, *yet* no one notices it. "In a dream, a vision of the night, When sound sleep falls on men, While they slumber in their beds, Then He opens the ears of men, And seals their instruction"

On the other hand, others know that the dreams are from God, but they fail to seek Him for any understanding of what they have seen in their dream. Understanding why God is speaking to us in a dream is just as relevant as what He is showing us in a dream. When we understand the purpose of a dream, it helps us have a better understanding of what God is saying to us. It also helps us understand how to respond to what is being said. Ultimately, our ability to even interpret a dream can shift as we begin to understand that our dreams have a specific purpose.

I put a short list together that deals with some of the most common reasons for our dreams.

WARNING

In a dream, the Lord can warn us of a situation that can transpire if we do not heed his warning. Warning dreams from God are quite common as the Lord is constantly trying to keep us from danger and on the right path. Warning dreams always require us to pray, but they may also require action on our part.

> **Matthew 2:11-12:** "And after entering the house, they saw the Child with Mary His mother; and they fell down and worshiped Him. Then, after opening their treasure chests, they presented to Him gifts [fit for a king, gifts] of gold, frankincense, and myrrh. [12] And having been warned [by God] in a dream not to go back to Herod, the magi left for their own country by another way."

> **Genesis 20:3-7:** "But God came to Abimelech in a dream of the night, and said to him, "Behold, you are a dead man because of the woman whom you have taken, for she is married." Now Abimelech had not come near her; and he said, "Lord, will You slay a nation, even *though* blameless? "Did he not himself say to me, 'She is my sister'? And she herself said, 'He is my brother.' In the integrity of my heart and the innocence of my hands I have done this." Then God said to him in the dream, "Yes, I know that in the integrity of your heart you have done this, and I also kept you from sinning against Me; therefore I did not let you touch her. "Now therefore, restore the man's wife, for he is a prophet, and he will pray for you and you will live. But if you do not restore *her,* know that you shall surely die, you and all who are yours."

D'Andrea Bolden

FORESIGHT

Some dreams reveal to us things that are to come. Whether literal or symbolic, dreams that reveal the future are very important. Depending on the context, prayer can alter the outcome of what has been revealed with some dreams; and others are just God showing you for you to be aware and prepared and prayer will not change the outcome of the dream. In either case, God is sovereign.

> **Judges 7:13-21:** " Gideon arrived just as a man was telling a friend his dream. "I had a dream," he was saying. "A round loaf of barley bread came tumbling into the Midianite camp. It struck the tent with such force that the tent overturned and collapsed." His friend responded, "This can be nothing other than the sword of Gideon son of Joash, the Israelite. God has given the Midianites and the whole camp into his hands." When Gideon heard the dream and its interpretation, he bowed down and worshiped. He returned to the camp of Israel and called out, "Get up! The LORD has given the Midianite camp into your hands." Dividing the three hundred men into three companies, he placed trumpets and empty jars in the hands of all of them, with torches inside. "Watch me," he told them. "Follow my lead. When I get to the edge of the camp, do exactly as I do. When I and all who are with me blow our trumpets, then from all around the camp blow yours and shout, 'For the LORD and for Gideon.'" Gideon and the hundred men with him reached the edge of the camp at the beginning of the middle watch, just after they had changed the guard. They blew their trumpets and broke the jars that were in their hands. The three companies blew the trumpets and smashed the jars. Grasping the torches in their left hands and holding in

their right hands the trumpets they were to blow, they shouted, "A sword for the LORD and for Gideon!" While each man held his position around the camp, all the Midianites ran, crying out as they fled.

Daniel 2:28: "But there is a God in heaven that revealeth secrets, **and maketh known to the king Nebuchadnezzar what shall be in the latter days**. Thy dream, and the visions of thy head upon thy bed, are these;"

INSTRUCTION

The Lord will plainly give us instructions in dreams. There are times that the Lord will plainly give you instruction that, if followed, will yield favorable results. Obeying God and following His instruction will never cause us to fail.

Job 33:15: "In a dream, in a vision of the night, when deep sleep falleth upon men, in slumberings upon the bed; Then he openeth the ears of men, and sealeth their instruction,

Genesis 31:24-26: "God came to Laban the Aramean in a dream of the night and said to him, Be careful that you do not speak to Jacob either good or bad."

SHOW US OURSELVES

A lot of people that have dreams, regardless of "who" they see in the dreams, it is still about them. God can sometimes show us other people as they can be likened to us in some way. A lot of people will find that their dreams are for them.

Their dreams might be to show them the state of their hearts, areas requiring deliverance, disobedience, pride, sin and other things that must be dealt with. We never want to go through life blinded by our own heart and ignorant of our own spiritual state. If ever God shows you something about yourself in a dream, He is trying to get your attention for your own benefit.

> **Daniel 4:9-18:** "I said, "Belteshazzar, chief of the magicians, I know that the spirit of the holy gods is in you, and no mystery is too difficult for you. Here is my dream; interpret it for me. These are the visions I saw while lying in bed: I looked, and there before me stood a tree in the middle of the land. Its height was enormous. The tree grew large and strong and its top touched the sky; it was visible to the ends of the earth. Its leaves were beautiful, its fruit abundant, and on it was food for all. Under it the wild animals found shelter, and the birds lived in its branches; from it every creature was fed. "In the visions I saw while lying in bed, I looked, and there before me was a holy one, a messenger, coming down from heaven. He called in a loud voice: 'Cut down the tree and trim off its branches; strip off its leaves and scatter its fruit. Let the animals flee from under it and the birds from its branches. But let the stump and its roots, bound with iron and bronze, remain in the ground, in the grass of the field.
> " 'Let him be drenched with the dew of heaven, and let him live with the animals among the plants of the earth. Let his mind be changed from that of a man and let him be given the mind of an animal, till seven times pass by for him." 'The decision is announced by messengers, the holy ones declare the verdict, so that the living may know that the Most High is sovereign over all kingdoms on earth and gives them to anyone he wishes and sets over them the

lowliest of people.' "This is the dream that I, King Nebuchadnezzar, had. Now, Belteshazzar, tell me what it means, for none of the wise men in my kingdom can interpret it for me. But you can, because the spirit of the holy gods is in you."

IMPARTATION & VISITATION

Just as in the Bible, some of our dreams can seem more like an encounter than anything else. You might even wake up from a dream crying and speaking in tongues. These are dreams where we might receive impartation and visitation. I have had dreams where I could feel the presence of the Lord so strong that it shook me to my core. I have also had dreams where I received powerful prophetic utterances and impartation.

> **Genesis 28:10-22:** "Now Jacob left Beersheba [never to see his mother again] and traveled toward Haran. And he came to a certain place and stayed overnight there because the sun had set. Taking one of the stones of the place, he put it under his head and lay down there [to sleep]. He dreamed that there was a ladder (stairway) placed on the earth, and the top of it reached [out of sight] toward heaven; and [he saw] the angels of God ascending and descending on it [going to and from heaven]. And behold, the LORD stood above *and* around him and said, "I am the LORD, the God of Abraham your [father's] father and the God of Isaac; I will give to you and to your descendants the land [of promise] on which you are lying. Your descendants shall be as [countless as] the dust of the earth, and you shall spread abroad to the west and the east and the north and the south; and all the families (nations) of the earth shall be blessed through you and your

descendants. Behold, I am with you and will keep [careful watch over you and guard] you wherever you may go, and I will bring you back to this [promised] land; for I will not leave you until I have done what I have promised you." Then Jacob awoke from his sleep and he said, "Without any doubt the LORD is in this place, and I did not realize it." So he was afraid and said, "How fearful *and* awesome is this place! This is none other than the house of God, and this is the gateway to heaven."

I Kings 3:5-15: "At Gibeon the LORD appeared to Solomon during the night in a dream, and God said, "Ask for whatever you want me to give you." Solomon answered, "You have shown great kindness to your servant, my father David, because he was faithful to you and righteous and upright in heart. You have continued this great kindness to him and have given him a son to sit on his throne this very day. "Now, LORD my God, you have made your servant king in place of my father David. But I am only a little child and do not know how to carry out my duties. Your servant is here among the people you have chosen, a great people, too numerous to count or number. So give your servant a discerning heart to govern your people and to distinguish between right and wrong. For who is able to govern this great people of yours?" The Lord was pleased that Solomon had asked for this. So God said to him, "Since you have asked for this and not for long life or wealth for yourself, nor have asked for the death of your enemies but for discernment in administering justice, I will do what you have asked. I will give you a wise and discerning heart, so that there will never have been anyone like you, nor will there ever be. Moreover, I will give you what you have not asked for—both wealth and honor—so that in your lifetime you will have no equal among kings. And if you walk in obedience to me and keep my decrees and commands as David your father did, I will give you a long life." Then Solomon awoke—and he realized it had been a dream."

COMFORT

The Lord always knows what we need, and many times He will release comfort to us when we need it most. Sometimes the loss of a loved one is hard on us and the Lord might give you a comforting dream that gives you a peace concerning the loss of your loved one. You could be stressed about something and the Lord could show you something in a dream that breaks the power of worry and releases a peace in your heart.

> **Matthew 1:20:** "But after he had considered this, an angel of the Lord appeared to him in a dream and said, "Joseph son of David, do not be afraid to take Mary home as your wife, because what is conceived in her is from the Holy Spirit."

REVEAL SECRETS

God can release secrets and mysteries to man in the form of dreams. Things that have been forgotten, or that have yet to materialize, can be unveiled in a dream.

> **Daniel 2:28:** "But there is a God in heaven that revealeth secrets, and maketh known to the king Nebuchadnezzar what shall be in the latter days. Thy dream, and the visions of thy head upon thy bed, are these"

GET OUR ATTENTION

If you saw that your child was about to walk in front of a speeding train, you would do what you could to prevent this. When we are on the wrong path and in a dangerous place God will sometimes get our attention in a dream. These are typically dreams that are uncomfortable yet unforgettable; frightening yet sobering all at the same time.

> **Job 7:14:** "Then You scare me with dreams and terrify me with visions"
>
> **Matthew 27:19:** "While he was sitting on the judgment seat, his wife sent him a message, saying, "Have nothing to do with that righteous Man; for last night I suffered greatly in a dream because of Him."

Highlights

- Your prophetic dreams have a purpose

- God does not give you dreams void of purpose

- The purpose of our dreams will vary

- Understanding the purpose of a dream helps with proper interpretation

Purpose

/ˈpərpəs/

(noun) 1. the reason for which something is done or created or for which something exists.

Ref: Dictionary.com

Types of Dreams-4

I want to ensure that people understand that there is diversity in dreams. The purpose, source, and type of dream all matter if we are going to understand the dream realm. One of the most misunderstood aspects about dreams is that all dreams are not the same and are not meant to be lumped into one big pile. We need wisdom and discernment in order to recognize the types of dreams that we are having, as this is directly connected to the source. I cannot emphasize enough that all dreams are not the same, and all dreams are not from God.

PROPHETIC DREAMS

I personally define prophetic dreams as dreams that come directly from the Lord. This is important to understand because all dreams are not from God, nor do they have any spiritual benefit. In order to simplify prophetic dreams, I compartmentalize them into two categories. The first category is literal dreams, and when I refer to literal prophetic dreams, these are dreams that require little to no interpretation. These are dreams where what is seen and heard is to be taken literally. The second category is prophetic dreams that are symbolic. These are the dreams that typically require interpretation. The message and full meaning is not as apparent, yet it is still God speaking through a dream.

Literal Dreams

Literal prophetic dreams are dreams where God is clearly and plainly releasing a prophetic message. Very often, these dreams require no interpretation in the meaning, but can sometimes still have elements in them that are symbolic and need interpretation. In other words, you might have a dream that is quite literal and what you see has or will happen, but sometimes there might be a few key things in the dream that still require interpretation. When this happens, the overall message of the dream is understood as the dream is very specific and straightforward. Typically, when a person has a dream that is literal, they remember the strong message that was shown in the dream and typically have few questions about what they saw. Personally, when I have literal dreams, I have noticed that they are not as "busy" as symbolic dreams and I usually do not experience any emotions during this type of dream. Literal dreams are like receiving an email in your sleep because it is coming straight to you and the message is clear. If you find that you are one that has dreams and what you see literally happens or comes to pass, you might be having dreams from the Lord that are literal dreams.

For example, I had a dream years ago about a woman finding out that her husband cheated on her and that she was going to leave him. Well, this situation is literally what took place in these individuals' lives. The people and the circumstances I saw in the dream literally happened and there was obviously no interpretation needed because God was showing me a dream that was literal in nature and not symbolic. Sometimes the Lord reveal these dreams to us so that we can pray. Everything we see in a dream that is literal is not always supposed to come to pass. God can reveal to us in a dream something that has not happened, but it will come to pass if we do not pray. Below, you will find biblical examples of literal dreams that were prophetic.

> **Genesis 31:24-26:** "God came to Laban the Aramean in a dream of the night and said to him, Be careful that you do not speak to Jacob either good or bad."

This is a great example of a literal dream. The Lord released a clear and strong message in the dream. There was nothing to interpret and Laban understood the purpose, the source, and the message of the dream. Literal dreams tend to leave the dreamer with a strong message that is easily understood. Some literal dreams could be a word of instruction, a warning, or a call to intercession, while others might show things that will eventually come to pass.

Symbolic Dreams

For many people, symbolic dreams are some of the most common prophetic dreams that they have. Symbolic dreams, unlike literal dreams, are sometimes a bit more complex to understand. Symbolic dreams are dreams that require interpretation, and interpretation comes from the Lord. All prophetic dreams are the language of God, but some dreams are not as easily understood. The deeper meaning of these dreams can be "hidden" from the dreamer. Although many people are sure that they have had a dream from the Lord, they are not always sure what any of it actually means. Understanding these types of dreams takes the wisdom of God to reveal the hidden meaning. Below are some biblical examples of symbolic dreams.

Genesis 40:8 – "And they said unto him, We have dreamed a dream, and there is no interpreter of it. And Joseph said unto them, Do not interpretations belong to God? tell me them, I pray you. And the chief butler told his dream to Joseph, and said to him, In my dream, behold, a vine was before me; And in the vine were three branches: and it was as though it budded, and her blossoms shot forth; and the clusters thereof brought forth ripe grapes: And Pharaoh's cup was in my hand: and I took the grapes, and pressed them into Pharaoh's cup, and I gave the cup into Pharaoh's hand. And Joseph said unto him, This is the interpretation of it: The three branches are three days: Yet within three days shall Pharaoh lift up thine head, and restore thee unto thy place: and thou shalt deliver Pharaoh's cup into his hand, after the former manner when thou wast his butler. But think on me when it shall be well with thee, and shew kindness, I pray thee, unto me, and make mention of me unto Pharaoh, and bring me out of this house: For indeed I was stolen away out of the land of the Hebrews: and here also have I done nothing that they should put me into the dungeon. When the chief baker saw that the interpretation was good, he said unto Joseph, I also was in my dream, and, behold, I had three white baskets on my head: And in the uppermost basket there was of all manner of bakemeats for Pharaoh; and the birds did eat them out of the basket upon my head. And Joseph answered and said, This is the interpretation thereof: The three baskets are three days: Yet within three days shall

Pharaoh lift up thy head from off thee, and shall hang thee on a tree; and the birds shall eat thy flesh from off thee. And it came to pass the third day, which was Pharaoh's birthday, that he made a feast unto all his servants: and he lifted up the head of the chief butler and of the chief baker among his servants. And he restored the chief butler unto his butlership again; and he gave the cup into Pharaoh's hand: But he hanged the chief baker: as Joseph had interpreted to them. Yet did not the chief butler remember Joseph, but forgat him.

OTHER DREAMS

As mentioned before all dreams are not from God. So, it is important to understand where our "other" dreams can come from. Why do you keep having dreams about intense sexual encounters? What is the reason you keep having dreams where you cannot move or speak? It is quintessential that we can discern the source of our dreams so that we are not attributing dreams to God that are definitely not from Him.

Soulish Dreams

Dreams can come from your heart, your subconscious, or even your trauma. It is a well-known fact that people that have been diagnosed with PTSD (Post-Traumatic Stress Disorder) are prone to have reoccurring dreams of the traumatic event. This is important to understand, because people have confused soulish dreams with unpleasant dreams from God or even dreams that are demonic.

The Dream Realm: Unlock, Interpret, and Govern Your Dreams

When we do not explain to people that the issues and flaws of their heart can overflow into their dreams, they will not be prepared to understand or discern the source of the dreams. Dreams coming from the soul can reveal our anger, our thoughts, our fears, or even our desires. Dreams coming from our soul can many times reveal what is going on in our heart and even that we need deliverance.

A person can strongly desire to marry a particular person and then begin having dreams of marrying that person. This happens when our strong desires manifest in our dreams. I have seen this happen to people. They refused to believe the dreams were not from God even after the person they desired got married to someone else. The state of our soul can absolutely affect our dreams. Your soul is made up of your mind, will, and emotions. So, your thoughts, emotions and desired action can manifest in your dreams.

We can also have dreams based on our day-to-day interactions and the things that entertain us. For instance, some people will dream about things they do on a regular basis, such as routine work tasks. It is also true that the music you listen to and the things you watch on TV can affect your dream life. I remember watching a SpongeBob marathon for hours at a time for multiple days. It should be no shock that I had a dream about SpongeBob because that show, and those images, are what my mind was focused on for hours non-stop. Soulish dreams do not necessarily have a spiritual benefit, although they can sometimes show us the dealings of our heart. Many things such as anger, sadness, or even fear can manifest in our dreams. Soulish dreams can convey the dealings of our heart and even the ponderings of our mind.

Demonic Dreams

As mentioned before, all dreams are not from God. In fact, some dreams are 100% demonic. This means that some dreams come from the enemy to inflict fear, seduce the dreamer into sin, cause confusion, and wreak havoc. Many prophetic people go through seasons where they are bombarded with constant demonic dreams and encounters.

I have seen how the spirit of fear can begin to grip a person that is dealing with demonic dreams where they are constantly being attacked. Some people will also experience demonic encounters where demons are manifesting themselves. These dreams and encounters can be frightening, tormenting and alarming for many believers. It is not uncommon for people to feel like they are being thrown around, unable to move, or scream during a dream or even wake up in a complete state of panic.

> **I John 4:18:** "There is no fear in love; but perfect love casts out fear, because fear involves torment. But he who fears has not been made perfect in love."

Some demonic dreams serve the purpose of luring people into sin. These dreams serve the purpose of weakening the will and some people have dreams about getting drunk or even getting high and in the dream and they can literally feel the sensation of intoxication or being high. Other people deal with X-rated dreams as the spirits of incubus and succubus manifest in their dreams. A lot of people are perplexed as to why they are having dreams that are filthy in content and their bodies in many cases will even climax.

Dreams that are demonic can make it apparent that we need to close some doors that were opened and are allowing demonic spirits legal grounds and access. Personal sin is an automatic way that doors can be opened. It is imperative to understand that doors can also be opened by our ancestors. This is where we must be humble enough to repent and renounce these things and close the door in Jesus' name. After waking up from demonic dreams, many have reported feeling extreme fear and anxiety, while others feel angry, deep sadness, or even confused.

Although every dream from God will not make us feel good especially when He is rebuking, correcting or even exposing our mess, it will never be confused with a dream from the enemy. Many have experienced demonic nightmares but even the Lord Himself can and will shake us up in a dream to get our attention if necessary.

Psychic Dreams

It is very important to understand that everyone that has dreams that seem spiritual in nature are not believers. Psychics, mediums, and even new age gurus have dreams too. Now, we all have the ability to have dreams as people and God is able to speak to everyone; but when people are involved in occult practices and they are using dreams to predict and foretell, those dreams are not coming from God. The reason I am mentioning this is because there are individuals that are releasing false prophetic dreams to believers. We must be careful in discerning the source of all dreams because some people are not receiving dreams that are prophetic and from God, but rather psychic dreams from familiar spirits.

Please understand that, as believers, we should never seek out psychics or go on psychic boards to get understanding of our dreams. As you see in the Bible, seeking out the magicians and those that operate in divination never works for receiving interpretation of a dream that comes from our Holy God.

Highlights

- All dreams are not from God

- Dreams from God can be literal or symbolic

-Dreams can come from our soul (desires, fears, trauma etc.)

-Some dreams are demonic

PART 2
INTERPRET YOUR DREAMS

Prophetic Symbols-5

Symbol: a mark or character used as a conventional representation of an object, function, or process

Ref: Oxford Dictionaries Online

In a symbolic dream, there will be prophetic symbolism throughout the dream. By prophetic symbolism, I am referring to all of the various components that give the dream meaning. Prophetic symbolism is like puzzle pieces, they all come together to make a puzzle. Prophetic symbolism is an area that is not always clear. Various sources will give you different meanings for the same prophetic symbol. This considered, how can we be sure of the meaning of the prophetic symbols in our dream?

One thing that needs to be considered, is how the prophetic symbols in your dream are relevant to you. Many times, when God shows us something, the meaning is tied to how it's relevant to us. This is why other sources will tell you that what you saw meant one thing, but you wholeheartedly disagree because you know in your spirit that is not what it meant in YOUR dream.

Many times, when people have symbolic dreams they can remember a lot of the prophetic elements in the dream. We have to learn how to look at all of the various prophetic symbols in our dreams to get the whole message of what God is saying.

Even in the Bible, there are great examples of dreams that were symbolic. Below is a passage from the book of Daniel that shares a symbolic dream from the Lord to Nebuchadnezzar. Nebuchadnezzar was a heathen king that served and worshipped many gods. Yet, we see that God was still able to speak a true word to him in the form of a dream.

> **Daniel 2:31-45:** "Your Majesty looked, and there before you stood a large statue—an enormous, dazzling statue, awesome in appearance. The head of the statue was made of pure gold, its chest and arms of silver, its belly and thighs of bronze, its legs of iron, its feet partly of iron and partly of baked clay. While you were watching, a rock was cut out, but not by human hands. It struck the statue on its feet of iron and clay and smashed them. Then the iron, the clay, the bronze, the silver and the gold were all broken to pieces and became like chaff on a threshing floor in the summer. The wind swept them away without leaving a trace. But the rock that struck the statue became a huge mountain and filled the whole earth.[6] "This was the dream, and now we will interpret it to the king. Your Majesty, you are the king of kings. The God of heaven has given you dominion and power and might and glory; in your hands he has placed all mankind and the beasts of the field and the birds in the sky. Wherever they live, he has made you ruler over them all. You are that head of gold. "After you, another kingdom will arise, inferior to yours. Next, a third kingdom, one of bronze, will rule over the whole earth. Finally, there will be a fourth kingdom, strong as iron—for iron breaks and smashes everything— and as iron breaks things to pieces, so it will crush and break all the others. Just as you saw that the feet and toes were partly of baked clay and partly of iron, so this will be a divided kingdom; yet it will have some of the strength of

iron in it, even as you saw iron mixed with clay. As the toes were partly iron and partly clay, so this kingdom will be partly strong and partly brittle. And just as you saw the iron mixed with baked clay, so the people will be a mixture and will not remain united, any more than iron mixes with clay. "In the time of those kings, the God of heaven will set up a kingdom that will never be destroyed, nor will it be left to another people. It will crush all those kingdoms and bring them to an end, but it will itself endure forever. This is the meaning of the vision of the rock cut out of a mountain, but not by human hands—a rock that broke the iron, the bronze, the clay, the silver and the gold to pieces. "The great God has shown the king what will take place in the future. The dream is true and its interpretation is trustworthy."

Because interpretation truly and only comes from the Lord, nobody was able to tell Nebuchadnezzar his dream and give interpretation except for Daniel. You can see how the Lord used things such as iron and clay and their natural characteristics such as strength to get his message across.

Below are some examples of types of prophetic symbols you might see in your dreams. This is by no means an exhaustive list, but here are a few categories and things that you might see in your dreams:

Language: Other languages that you speak, foreign known languages that you do not speak (i.e. Swahili, Russian, French, etc.)

People: Familiar and unfamiliar, family members and friends, clergy, strangers

Animals: Dogs, fish, cats, birds, wildcats, bears, frogs, lizards, insects, snakes, spiders, moles, elephants, zebras, pig, warthog

> [this is a very short list of animals because the list is far too long to include a small section in a dream book]

Jewelry: Crowns, rings, watches, bracelets, necklaces, earrings, broaches

Hair and clothing: Wig, hat, bald, sunglasses, long hair, short hair, beard, mustache, robe, pants, shorts, shirt, swimsuit, partially clothed, shoes, boots, coat, suit, socks, gloves, purse, wallet

Metals and stones: Diamonds, gemstones, gold, silver, platinum, iron

Nature and environment: Trees, bodies of water, clouds, wind, volcanoes, geysers, waterfalls, mountains, valleys, cliffs, peaks, vineyards, fruit trees, crops, gardens

Food and drink: Fruit, vegetables, meat, water, juice, alcohol, milk, coffee, tea

Smokes and drugs: Cigarettes, cigars, pipes, crack pipe, blunt, needles, powder, pills

Colors: Red, green, blue, yellow, orange, black, white, purple, pink, brown

Technology: Phone, camera, computer, laptop, tablet, apps, social media, email, printer

Land Vehicles: Car, snowmobiles, RTV, bike, motorcycle, bus, van, truck, train

Communication: Letter, postcard, email, voicemail, book, newspaper, magazine, telephone, text message, note, journal

Household items: Scale, mirror, washer and dryer, dishwasher, stove, fridge, freezer, microwave, coffee maker

Water Vehicles: Fishing boat, luxury boat, jet skis, submarine, kayak, floating device

Air Vehicles: Airplanes, fighter and bomber planes, helicopters, hot air balloons, rockets, etc.

Rooms in a house: Kitchen, bathroom, bedroom, living room, garage, basement, attic, walk-in closet

Weather: Sunny and pleasant, cloudy, dark and gloomy, storm, rain, tornado, earthquake, hurricane, snow, ice

Buildings: Bank, courtroom, skyscraper, hospital, museum, library, funeral home, store, church, school, office, prison/jail, psychiatric hospital

Location (Specific): Church, store, school, home, bank, airport, childhood home, place of employment, beach, heaven, hell

Location (Geographic): City, State, Country

The Dream Realm: Unlock, Interpret, and Govern Your Dreams

Numbers: 1, 2, 3, 4, 5, 6, 7, 8, 9, 10, 11, 12, 13, 20, 25, 30, 40, 50, 100, 1000

Activities: Cooking, cleaning, praying, running, swimming, singing, preaching/teaching, prophesying, casting out devils, studying, working, playing an instrument, playing a sport, exercising, driving, sleeping, writing, typing, watching TV, reading, talking, crying

Emotions: Happy, excited, worried, afraid, confused, angry, sorrowful, joyful

Dates and Times: Midnight, noon, day of the week, month, year

Furniture: Table, chairs, couch, bed, dresser, vanity, lamp, futon, desk, armoire, ottoman, recliner, bar stool, rocking chair, bench, bunk bed, baby crib, mattress, bookshelf, curio cabinet, coat rack

Toys: Board games, puzzles, toy cars/trains, dolls, doll house, rattles, teething rings, video games

Currency: Credit/debit card, coin money, paper money, ATM

Misc. Objects: windows, sink, engine, paper, pen, clock, lamp, wall, door, stairs, curtains, glasses, toys, fireplace

Interpretation
/ inˌtərprəˈtāSH(ə)n/

1. (noun) 1. the action of explaining the meaning of something.

Ref: Dictionary.com

Dream Interpretation-6

Interpretation: the action of explaining the meaning of something
Ref: Dictionary.com

By now, you have probably bought and read books on dream interpretation; this chapter is not going to deal with dream interpretation in the manner you have probably seen before. I am not going to lay out definitions for a plethora of common symbols in your dream, especially when people look at these definitions many times and feel like what they are looking for is missing. This chapter is simply about dream interpretation. If you are a Spirit-filled believer and God is speaking to you in dreams, He is more than able to unlock them and give you understanding of what He has shown you. Many dreams are like a wrapped gift; you know you have received something, but you have to open it to find out what it is.

Asking God for understanding of your dreams does not mean that you are a Joseph or a Daniel, or one who is highly skilled in interpretation. However, I do believe that as believers, we need to begin to seek God more for understanding. After having a dream, your first step should be quickly recording your dream (to avoid forgetting your dream) and prayer. You should not immediately ask someone for interpretation. I am not saying anything is wrong with ever asking people that are anointed in this area for assistance. But we cannot lean on people more than the Father. If a dream is God speaking to you, shouldn't you speak back to Him first? Many times, we do not want to take the time to pray because it is easier, and more convenient, to pull on someone else. But it is so important that we seek God first. It would be of great surprise to many of us the willingness and readiness God has when it comes to speaking back to us. God is so loving and compassionate towards us and He desires for us to be close to Him.

Dream interpretation simply allows you to take the dream that you saw and understand the meaning of it and even express the meaning in your own language. Remember that dreams are the language of God and we are taking it from one language so that it can be understood. According to the Bible, interpretation comes from the Lord. This is one of the most important things to understand as it relates to dream interpretation. God is the source of the dream, so He also holds the key to unlocking and understanding your dreams. The more it is understood that dreams are a language, the more we look into everything that makes up the dream. In the Bible, we see great examples of prophetic dreams and their interpretation. Two of these dreams were given to Kings that were not believers.

> **Genesis 40:8** "And they said unto him, We have dreamed a dream, and *there is* no interpreter of it. And Joseph said unto them, ***Do not interpretations belong* to God? tell me *them*, I pray you.**"

That is the beauty of dreams; anyone can have a dream. We are all wired with the innate ability to hear from God in the form of dreams; this holds true even for people that are unsaved. I can remember having dreams from the time I was a kid, and no one ever taught me what a dream was. I just woke up and knew that I had a dream. Even with my own children, they started to come and tell me that they had dreams without me ever explaining to them anything about dreams.

Dreams and interpretation is an area that breeds a lot of confusion as it quickly becomes muddy waters. One reason is that many like to approach dreams from a one size fits all perspective instead of an individualized approach. Your God-given dreams are customized for you. God speaks to you in a way that you can recognize. So, two people can be strong dreamers and never dream about the same thing. Or God can even speak a similar message to two people and their dreams are nothing alike. Just as our DNA is unique, so are our dreams and the way God speaks to us.

When parents have more than one child, they understand that they need to deal with each child differently because their personalities are very different. God, in His infinite wisdom, does not speak to all of His people the same way for the same reason. God, in His infinite wisdom, speaks to us for different reasons, to show us different things in our dreams.

Let's begin to look closer at a few things that are quite relevant in our dreams.

PEOPLE: Sometimes the people you see in dreams are people that you recognize, and sometimes they are unfamiliar faces. God sometimes will show us different people in our dream and the dream can still be about us because the other person has a likeness to us in some way.

Sometimes other people in our dream are speaking to us and other times, they are silent.

I had several dreams about my grandmother who had already passed away, and in the dreams, I was always in my childhood church sitting on a pew. My grandmother would walk up towards me and drop a small white cloth and I would pick it up. In one dream, after I picked it up, what started off as a small white cloth grew to the size of a large white sheet. There was great rejoicing and I began to speak in tongues. The Lord showed me through these dreams, and it was confirmed by other prophets, that the anointing that rested upon my grandmother's life was passed on to me.

LOCATION [Country, State, City, Building, Room]: The location of your dream is very important. Depending on the purpose of your dream, the location can deal with the state of your heart, your assignment, your past, or even your future. Seeing yourself in different countries could possibly mean that the Lord is showing you that He is taking you to new places, or that you might even travel there; or you could have an international anointing and grace on your life.

Years ago, I had repetitive dreams about rushing to the airport to fly to Germany, but whenever I got to the airport I could not leave because I did not have a passport [access, authority, etc.]. After I kept having this dream, I prayed and asked God to show me what I needed to do, and one day I randomly grabbed my Bible and a postcard fell at my feet advertising how and when to get your expedited passport. After I went and got my passport, I stopped having those dreams. Instead I would have dreams of arriving at the airport boarding the plane and taking off and soaring.

EMOTIONS: [Your emotions during and after the dream] - Emotions are very relevant to your dream and they can greatly assist in understanding your dream. If you are waking up from a dream excited or even speaking in tongues, that speaks volumes. Some people will wake up from a dream sad and weeping, and sometimes God is moving on them to pray. Your emotions are so important as it relates to proper interpretation. If you had a dream that you won $1,000,000 but you immediately felt a heavy sadness, or even anger, that lets you know that there is more to the interpretation than just the possibility of getting a large sum of money.

The reason why all the prophetic symbolism in your dream is important is because together these types of dream elements are used to convey a message. But, what do they all mean? A lot of people end up having their dreams incorrectly interpreted because a lot of times, the elements and symbols in the dream that we see have a meaning that is relevant to us. In other words, a person that is skilled in dream interpretation might say that high level of water means that you are being submerged in the spirit of God. But in actuality, to you, it really means that you are overwhelmed and drowning. There will be times that God will use certain elements in your dreams because of the significance it has in your life. For one person, a doll might represent immaturity or being childish, but to you, it can be tied to memories from your childhood that bring you peace and comfort. Therefore, in that dream God was not trying to tell you that you are immature; He was actually trying to comfort you.

LANGUAGE: It might not seem insignificant, but language is very significant in your dreams. The dream itself is a part of God's language; but languages are being communicated in your dreams. This is very important, especially for those that speak multiple languages. Once you have learned an additional language, and it gets into your subconscious mind, you will find it can begin to manifest in your dreams.

For example, I had a dream years ago that I was outside and it was raining and I was walking towards a man that did not look familiar. Once I got close enough to the man, he looked at me and said "Kennst du mich?" (English translation: "Do you know me?") I did not know the man, and at that time, it quickly came to my mind that I really did not know Jesus like I should. That dream was a wake-up call to let me know that I needed to really know Jesus for myself. What was said in the dream stuck with me and made more of an impact in German than it would have ever made in English!! God always knows how to get our attention!!

I also had a dream where I saw a group of brown-skinned people. They had dark hair and were clearly in another country. In this dream, The Lord started to speak a prophetic message to me, but I could also hear that the people in the dream were speaking fluent Spanish because I could recognize the language. This helped me to better understand what the Lord spoke audibly in the dream because I knew what people God was revealing to me because the language helped solidify this.

Understanding that many times the elements and symbols we see in our dreams hold a meaning that is relevant to us can help explain why many people are frustrated about dreams and interpretation. Many people have sought out individuals for help with dream interpretation and they walk away scratching their head because it does not bear witness with their spirit. When the interpretation of a dream is correct, you will know because it will agree with your spirit and you will have the feeling of confirmation. You do not have to accept an interpretation of your dream if you feel that it is incorrect. Too many people have allowed others to force their interpretation on them.

It is important that believers begin to inquire of the Lord for interpretation of their dreams. Although we see dream interpretation in the Bible, the people receiving interpretation were not always believers. There are a lot of anointed people that are skilled in the area of interpretation, but it is unhealthy to automatically reach out and seek assistance from people before taking the time to pray. We do not want to become dependent on anyone other than the Holy Spirit. This is not to say that it is wrong to ask a proven vessel for help understanding your dreams. But if your dreams are coming from God, who better to give you understanding than the source? In fact, the Lord wants to speak to us many times about what He has shown us in our dreams. And because He is giving us the dreams, that proves that He desires to speak to us. It would be rude for you to call me and leave a message on my voicemail and instead of calling you back to get clarification, I call a friend and ask them what you meant. Basically, no one knows your dreams like the one that is giving them to you in the first place.

BENEFITS OF INTERPRETATION

Proper interpretation will allow us to understand clearly what God has spoken in a dream. The more we understand fully what He has spoken in a dream, the more we are able to understand His language. Interpretation can also allow God to give us strategy. We can see that in Genesis; once Joseph gave the interpretation of the dream, he also knew what to do. Interpreting the dream and knowing that a famine was coming in 7 years was a wonderful but having the wisdom and strategy to know what to do was even better. The same is true with Gideon overhearing a dream and interpretation in Judges the 7th chapter. Once Gideon heard the dream and interpretation, he bowed down and worshipped. What he did next proved that God gave him strategy and wisdom because no one in their right mind, for no reason, would gather 300 soldiers with trumpets and empty jars and head to the camp of their enemy.

> **Judges 7:15-22:** "When Gideon heard the dream and its interpretation, he bowed down and worshiped. He returned to the camp of Israel and called out, "Get up! The LORD has given the Midianite camp into your hands." Dividing the three hundred men into three companies, he placed trumpets and empty jars in the hands of all of them, with torches inside. "Watch me," he told them. "Follow my lead. When I get to the edge of the camp, do exactly as I do. When I and all who are with me blow our trumpets, then from all around the camp blow yours and shout, 'For the LORD and for Gideon.'" Gideon and the hundred men with him reached the edge of the camp at the beginning of the middle watch, just after they had changed the guard. They blew their trumpets and

broke the jars that were in their hands. The three companies blew the trumpets and smashed the jars. Grasping the torches in their left hands and holding in their right hands the trumpets they were to blow, they shouted, "A sword for the LORD and for Gideon!" While each man held his position around the camp, all the Midianites ran, crying out as they fled. When the three hundred trumpets sounded, the LORD caused the men throughout the camp to turn on each other with their swords. The army fled to Beth Shittah toward Zererah as far as the border of Abel Meholah near Tabbath."

EXPLORING DREAM INTERPRETATION

Let's take a look at a familiar dream that most have heard about in the Bible. This is Pharaoh's dream and the interpretation that came through Joseph.

Genesis 41:1-32 "When two full years had passed, Pharaoh had a dream: He was standing by the Nile, [2] when out of the river there came up seven cows, sleek and fat, and they grazed among the reeds. [3] After them, seven other cows, ugly and gaunt, came up out of the Nile and stood beside those on the riverbank. [4] And the cows that were ugly and gaunt ate up the seven sleek, fat cows. Then Pharaoh woke up. [5] He fell asleep again and had a second dream: Seven heads of grain, healthy and good, were growing on a single stalk. [6] After them, seven other heads of grain sprouted—thin and scorched by the east wind. [7] The thin heads of grain swallowed up the seven healthy, full heads. Then Pharaoh woke up; it had been a dream. [8] In the morning his mind was troubled, so he sent for all the magicians and wise men of Egypt. Pharaoh told them his dreams, but no one could interpret them for him.

⁹ Then the chief cupbearer said to Pharaoh, "Today I am reminded of my shortcomings. ¹⁰ Pharaoh was once angry with his servants, and he imprisoned me and the chief baker in the house of the captain of the guard. ¹¹ Each of us had a dream the same night, and each dream had a meaning of its own. ¹² Now a young Hebrew was there with us, a servant of the captain of the guard. We told him our dreams, and he interpreted them for us, giving each man the interpretation of his dream. ¹³ And things turned out exactly as he interpreted them to us: I was restored to my position, and the other man was impaled." ¹⁴ So Pharaoh sent for Joseph, and he was quickly brought from the dungeon. When he had shaved and changed his clothes, he came before Pharaoh. ¹⁵ Pharaoh said to Joseph, "I had a dream, and no one can interpret it. But I have heard it said of you that when you hear a dream you can interpret it." ¹⁶ "I cannot do it," Joseph replied to Pharaoh, "but God will give Pharaoh the answer he desires." ¹⁷ Then Pharaoh said to Joseph, "In my dream I was standing on the bank of the Nile, ¹⁸ when out of the river there came up seven cows, fat and sleek, and they grazed among the reeds. ¹⁹ After them, seven other cows came up—scrawny and very ugly and lean. I had never seen such ugly cows in all the land of Egypt. ²⁰ The lean, ugly cows ate up the seven fat cows that came up first. ²¹ But even after they ate them, no one could tell that they had done so; they looked just as ugly as before. Then I woke up. ²² "In my dream I saw seven heads of grain, full and good, growing on a single stalk. ²³ After them, seven other heads sprouted—withered and thin and scorched by the east wind. ²⁴ The thin heads of grain swallowed up the seven good heads. I told this to the magicians, but none of them could explain it to me." ²⁵ Then Joseph said to Pharaoh, "The dreams of Pharaoh are one and the same.

God has revealed to Pharaoh what he is about to do. [26] The seven good cows are seven years, and the seven good heads of grain are seven years; it is one and the same dream. [27] The seven lean, ugly cows that came up afterward are seven years, and so are the seven worthless heads of grain scorched by the east wind: They are seven years of famine. [28] "It is just as I said to Pharaoh: God has shown Pharaoh what he is about to do. [29] Seven years of great abundance are coming throughout the land of Egypt, [30] but seven years of famine will follow them. Then all the abundance in Egypt will be forgotten, and the famine will ravage the land. [31] The abundance in the land will not be remembered, because the famine that follows it will be so severe. [32] The reason the dream was given to Pharaoh in two forms is that the matter has been firmly decided by God, and God will do it soon."

Pharaoh actually had two dreams (repetitive dream) and they had the exact same interpretation. The Lord was trying to make sure His message was received. Below I am breaking the dream down to help make the interpretation a bit plainer.

Location: By the Nile

Emotions: Troubled

Numbers: 7

People: Pharaoh

Animals: 7 Cows fat and sleek; ugly and gaunt

Other: 7 heads of grain healthy and good; scorched

7 Years of plenty

7 fat and sleek cows eating the reeds. In the Bible, cattle were always a form of currency and wealth. So, to have fat cows means that they are well fed and there is grassland (pasture) for them to graze. They were plump and healthy-looking cows, which meant they were well cared for, fed, and hydrated.

7 heads of grain, healthy and good. In order to have healthy grain, they have to be properly watered and cared for in order to grow correctly. The right conditions would have to be in place for the crops to grow and be healthy.

7 Years of famine

7 ugly and gaunt cows were standing on the riverbanks. For an animal to be gaunt, it would mean that they are unhealthy and in a state of hunger. If the cows were hungry, this essentially meant there was no pasture or the like for them to graze on.

7 heads of grain scorched by the east wind. Scorched crops were a sign of famine caused by crop failure that could be due to heat and a lack of water. This would cause a food shortage in the land. In both dreams, the cows and grain heads that represented famine came after he saw the healthy ones. This is why with the interpretation, it is 7 years of famine after 7 years of plenty.

MATURING IN DREAM INTERPRETATION

As Spirit-filled believers, God can give us understanding of what He is speaking to us in dreams. When God speaks to us in dreams, we are able to pray and ask Him for interpretation on our own. A lot of people will even find that their dream life expands, and their understanding expands as they spend time with God. There are some people that are not growing prophetically in the area of dreams because they are dependent on man and not God. Spend time with God, pray and ask questions about what He is speaking to you in dreams. We cannot grow in this area of the prophetic if we do not study, pray, and spend time with God.

Please note that, with the interpretation, God also gave Joseph the wisdom to know what to do so that they could survive during the 7 years of famine. We do not want to just know we had a dream and get interpretation, but we need to know what to do after we understand what the Lord has spoken to us in the form of a dream. Always remember, our dreams and their interpretation are subject to the Word of God. In other words, your dreams and their interpretation should never go against the written word of God. The Word of God is our guide and our boundaries. This matters, because if the dream is truly from God, it will never in any way go against God's written word. God and His Word are one (John 1:1).

Highlights

-Interpretation comes from God

-Pray before asking others to help with your dream

-If your dream is God speaking to you, HE should be the first one you ask for help to understand your dream

-Dreams and interpretation are subject to the written word of God.

-Interpretation of a dream and having understanding can unlock strategy and the wisdom of God to know what to do.

Scope
/ skōp/

1. (noun) the extent of the area or subject matter that something deals with or to which it is relevant.

Ref: Dictionary.com

Dream Scope-7

Scope: the extent of the area or subject matter that something deals with or to which it is relevant
Ref: Dictionary.com

The scope of your dreams is important so that you understand how to respond and reply to your dream. If you had a dream in which God released a warning, how do you know who the warning is to and how to handle what he shared? Some people will find that their dreams are always only for them. These are typically dreams where God is showing us our flaws, things to pray for, warnings, instructions, or even correction.

Other people have dreams concerning groups of people such as their family or church. Yet another group of people will have dreams for regions of people or even nations.

Do not be close-minded in believing that all of your dreams are always 100% for you. Thinking in this manner can cause you to miss the full meaning of your prophetic dream. In other words, you have to know who your dream is for. Pharaoh's dream about the famine was for more than just himself because the famine would affect nations. By Joseph interpreting the dream and releasing the wisdom to have a strategy, nations survived and it all started with a dream.

For myself, I dream a lot about world leaders, global events, and church leaders. This does not mean that God never shows me a dream concerning myself, my family or anything of that nature. But, I am also conscious and aware that God deals with me about governmental and international affairs.

I cannot overemphasize the need for prayer to really grow and mature in the area of dreams. It is imperative to understand that many times after a dream, our immediate response needs to be prayer. Prayer helps us become more disciplined and also more connected and in tune with God as it relates to our dreams.

Highlights

-Some people only have dreams pertaining to themselves

-Some people have dreams that pertain to other people in their life such as family and friends

-Some dreamers will have dreams about their local church and other believers.

- Some dreamers with strong prophetic calls will have dreams about nations, global leaders, and major events.

Journal
/ jûr′nəl**/**

1. (noun) A personal record of occurrences, experiences, and reflections kept on a regular basis; a diary.

Ref: freedictionary.com

Journaling Prophetic Dreams -8

One of the first things that I began to do without ever being told was recording my dreams. I believe this is what helped me become more disciplined and this helped me become strengthened in discerning the voice of the Lord. Journaling allowed me to see my dreams written out so that I could continue to pray about what the Lord had shown me. Journaling also allowed me to have a way to keep track of the dates that I had various dreams and it allowed me to review what God had already spoken.

Journaling helps you write down the dream so that you do not forget it. Although there are some dreams that really stick with us, journaling will allow you to revisit the dream on paper. This way, if you forget some details, it is already recorded. Journaling your dreams is powerful. Sometimes when we see a dream again we can get a better understanding. Many times, as you go back through the details of a dream, revelation and insight might come and overlooked details will pop out at you. Sometimes, we get more clarity and understanding of a dream over time. Recording your dreams and writing down the date also allows you to see what God said and when HE said it. This is important because sometimes we might find patterns in our dreams. For instance, you might find that your dreams about yourself come to pass after 6 years. Or you might find that you only dream once a week or once a month. Recording the dates of your dreams also allows you to recognize if the Lord deals with you in dreams during certain times of the year.

When I first recognized that God was constantly speaking to me in dreams, I would write letters or even ask God questions by writing it down in my journal and He would respond in a dream when I went to sleep at night. Journaling really helped me mature in the prophetic and helped me unlock, interpret, and govern my own dreams. I learned quickly how God speaks to me in dreams and also how to respond to what He was saying. Although I record a lot of my dreams now via email or technology, I still love writing in my journals. Writing in journals is still relevant because it allows you to be more creative and expressive as you record your prophetic dreams.

Many times, as we are recording our prophetic dreams and pray to the Lord, we will put scriptures with our dreams. A lot of people will find that dreams and visions are the entrance to the prophetic for them. Further, people will also use their phone to record a prophetic utterance that has been released over their lives.

It is both imperative and wise for us to value the word of the Lord released through dreams, and ensure that we are recording them. Some of the most relevant prophetic messages released in my life have come in the form of dreams. We can miss a lot of revelation, insight and instruction if we ignore, or do not take the time to understand what God is speaking to us in dreams. If you do not write your dreams down quickly, you are prone to forget them. Since journaling my dreams, I have noticed a very strong maturation in the area of managing and understanding prophetic dreams.

QUICK NOTE: I thought it was very important to have an interactive journal that accompanies this book. This is to ensure that you are able to not only record your dreams but also apply what you have read in this book. If you have not already, be sure to purchase the matching interactive journal that goes along with this book.

Highlights

-Recording your dreams allows you to go back and see what God has already spoken.

-Journaling your dreams allows you to look back at dreams and sometimes you will find that the dream and your understanding of it will unfold more over time.

-Recording your dreams with a date allows you to see what God said and when He said it.

PART 3
THE DREAM REALM

Innovation

/ˌinəˈvāSH(ə)n/

(noun) 1. the introduction of something new, 2. a new idea, method, or device

Ref: dictionary.com

D'Andrea Bolden

Dreams + Innovators-9

We serve the God of creation and He created the universe and everything in it because He is the greatest to ever do it. The creative nature of God is what allows us to also be creative.

> "In the beginning, God created the heavens and the earth." **Genesis 1:1**

> And, "You, Lord, laid the foundation of the earth in the beginning, and the heavens are the work of your hands" **Hebrews 1:10**

Although we are all created in His image, some people are stronger in some areas than others. This is why some people are very creative and they are always working on creating something new or the next big thing. Individuals that are always introducing something new are not only creatives, but they are also innovators. An innovator is someone that creates and introduces new products, methods and ideas.

Some of the most creative people I know are also strong dreamers. Many times, in a dream they will see and hear and experience what they are to create ahead of time. It is not uncommon for prophetic creatives to get their inspiration to create something new from a dream. New songs, new inventions, new books, new art, new fashion designs, new culinary concepts, new business ideas, new architectural designs, new graphic ideas, and so forth, many times start as a dream. By nature, creatives are innovators automatically, because they are always creating something new.

It is imperative for creatives to understand how God will speak to them through dreams in order to give them new downloads for them to create. For example, prophetic artists many times will "see" a picture or finished concept in a dream or vision, and then use their gift of art to create what the Lord showed them. Musicians, singers, and songwriters might hear new songs, whether it's the music, the lyrics, or both, but they will skillfully use their musical talent to create the new song that they heard in a dream.

Did you know that some of the world's greatest inventions, books, and ideas started as a dream? There are countless stories about inventions, and even books, that were created after the concept was revealed in a dream. Sadly, some of these individuals were oblivious to the fact that the source of many of these powerful dreams was God. This is definitely not always the case, but we can still see how powerful dreams can be in the lives of everyday people. Through these dreams and visions come art, new technology, songs, business ideas, books, poetry, new designs, cutting edge ideas, and even scientific breakthroughs. [1]

Innovation + Inventions That Came From A Dream. Please note that these dreams **are not** said to be from God. However, I put this list together to simply show how innovation and inventions can flow through dreams.

Madame C.J. Walker had issues with her hair falling out. In a dream, it was revealed to her what ingredient to mix up and put in her hair. To her surprise, not only did it work, but her hair was growing in very fast. She decided to sell this as a product and she eventually became the first black millionaire in America.

Elias Howe had an issue with creating an operable sewing machine. In a dream, he saw what he needed to do in order to solve the problem he had with the needle. This allowed him to create an operable sewing machine.

Robert Louis Stevenson is the author of Dr. Jekyll and Mr. Hyde. He describes how he writes these books as the plot comes to him in a series of dreams. He stated that his dreams were very vivid and entertaining, and that he would dream about an entire storyline for a book.

Beatles song Yesterday came to group member Paul McCartney in a dream. The song became stuck in his head, but he was not convinced that he had a brand-new song from a dream. After ensuring that the song was an original the Beatles released the song.

Srinivasa Ramanujan was a mathematical genius who would get insight and even new formulas in his dreams. Sometimes, he would see a hand writing and he would get up and verify the formulas that were in his dream. He discovered the infinite series of pi. He had little to no formal training in math but states his success is related to his dreams.

Stephen King is a world-renowned author and he shared how his inspiration for writing Mystery and other books came to him in a dream.

Friedrich August Kekulé von Stradonitz is a figure in the history of chemistry and he discovered that the shape of benzene, unlike many other molecules, was not linear. This discovery came to him in a dream. This breakthrough was monumental for the world of chemistry.

Dmitry Mendeleyev saw the entire periodic table in a dream. After working tirelessly for several days, he took a quick break to nap. While he was asleep, he saw a table with all the elements arranged properly. He quickly recorded this, and it was a major contribution to the world of chemistry.

Dr. James Watson had a dream that helped bring understanding to the structure of DNA. He had a dream that caused him to consider double helix as the structure for DNA.

Niehls Bohr had a dream that revealed the structure of the atom. He saw electrons spinning around the atom. After having this dream, he was confident it was correct. He went on to conduct a series of testing to verify that this was in fact accurate and true. He later received a Nobel prize.

Otto Loewi had a dream about an experiment that showed him that nerve impulses were not electrical but chemical. He is also responsible for the discovery of acetylcholine. Acetylcholine is the neurotransmitter that promotes dreaming. He was eventually awarded a Nobel prize.

Highlights

-Some of the world's greatest innovations came from dreams.

-Prophetic artists and other creatives will create based off what they are seeing in dreams.

Sensory Impairment

/ˈsensərē imˈpermənt/

(noun) 1. is when one of your senses; sight, hearing, smell, touch, taste and spatial awareness, is not functioning normal but is impaired.

Dreams + Sensory Impairment -10

One population of people that tend to be left out as it relates to the prophetic is the blind and deaf community, or the sensory impaired. They are no less loved by God than anyone else. Therefore, He desires and can speak to them just like the rest of mankind. One thing to understand as it relates to those that are deaf or blind is that the brain has a way of compensating for the loss or lack of function of one's senses. This is why the brain will. in a sense, rewire itself in a way that the other senses are enhanced. A person that is sensory impaired will attest to the fact that the other senses are stronger. This is what enables people that are blind to use sound to "see" and they can move around like someone that can see with their two eyes. This technique is known as echolocation. Echolocation is a result of the accommodations that the brain has made to adjust to the sensory impairment.

The visually impaired use Braille and the hearing-impaired use sign language to speak because all people are created to communicate with others. When people are unable to communicate with other people, learning, social skills, and even mental health will be affected. Have you ever lost your voice and struggled for people to be able to understand what you are saying? The inability to be understood can happen a lot in the Christian community when there is a lack of people that "speak" the language of those that they are trying to communicate with. It is imperative that the faith-based community does not exclude the sensory impaired.

Dreams and the Sensory Impaired (Hearing & Vision)

There have been studies conducted on sensory impaired individuals to help bring insight to what the dream world is like for them. The ability of the brain to compensate for sensory impairments does not exclude dreams. Even though God-given dreams are spiritual and will pull on our spiritual senses, God is wise enough to keep our abilities the same in our dreams.

If a person went blind during childhood or later in life, they are prone to "seeing" in their dreams, but, over time, the sight in their dreams will begin to fade. However, if a person is born blind, they will not see in their dreams. This concept is the same for those that are born deaf or that lose hearing later in life. When it comes to dreams, people that are blind, or visually impaired, are more likely to have dreams with intensified sound, smell, taste, and feeling. Individuals with impairment of sight have shared dreams with strong winds, intense smells, and taste, loud booms, and other phenomena.

Whether a person was born deaf or went deaf later in life will ultimately dictate whether they "hear" in their dreams. People that are born deaf are not going to "hear" in their dreams. But they tend to have dreams that are visually heightened with bright vivid colors and strong impressions through what they are seeing and feeling. Many people that are hearing impaired have reported dreams where they automatically know what a person was saying in a dream. It is also not uncommon for those with visual and auditory impairment to have heightened smell in their dreams just like in their everyday lives. Those with sensory impairments are not forgotten by God.

You typically dream in the way you communicate in day-to-day life. A lot of deaf people that communicate via sign language have dreams where everyone in the dream can sign. There will also be heightened taste, touch, and smell. For many, however, the visual component of the dream will leave a very strong impression. Others have stated that there is no one talking but you "know" what the people are saying. Unfortunately, many have ascribed this to telepathy because they do not understand the language of God.

I think it is important to realize that in the faith-based community, we are overlooking people as if God doesn't speak to them, when He does. In many cases, barriers in communication can leave them open to be indoctrinated from a secular humanistic approach. Basically, because most Christians are not fluent in Braille or sign language, this population of people are prone to be taught things with no regard for God and His word.

We cannot empower believers and forget those that have sensory impairments. Yes, God can heal, but even when Jesus walked the earth, He did not heal everyone and raise everyone from the dead. God wants to raise up people that are visually impaired and are hearing impaired. They will then be able to minister to other people.

The inability to see and hear does not mean a person is deficient in intellect. You can have a sensory impairment and be as smart as Einstein. The inability to see or hear will not stop God from speaking to His people.

The Dream Realm: Unlock, Interpret, and Govern Your Dreams

Highlights

-God can and does speak to the sensory impaired.

-The senses that are enhance in everyday life are also enhanced in their dreams.

-People that are deaf and fluent in sign language tend to have dreams where the language is sign language, just like a person that is fluent in a spoken language tends to dream in the language that they speak.

Creative

/ krēˈādiv/

(adjective) 1. relating to or involving the imagination or original ideas, especially in the production of an artistic work.

(noun) 2. a person who is creative, typically in a professional context.

Ref: dictionary.com

Dreams + Children -11

When we read the Bible, we can see that God has always used dreams and visions to communicate with man. Many times, when God begins to "awaken" prophetic people, they begin to have dreams and visions. In fact, a lot of prophetic people begin to have strong dreams and visions early on in life. This is why it is important to realize that God can and does speak to our children. Just like the prophet Samuel, most children have to be told that their dreams are coming from God. One of the most amazing aspects is that God speaks to children in a way that they can understand.

I have found over the years that small children will have dreams that incorporate elements of good and bad from their favorite cartoons. God shows them things that they can recognize, understand, and that they have language for. It would make no sense for God to show a dream about a pending national disaster to a 2-year-old child. More than likely, they would not understand what they saw in the dream.

I can remember with both of my children, they began to dream around the age of 3. Both of my children came to me to tell me that they had a dream without me ever talking to them about dreams or explaining what a dream is. There is a variety of reasons why God speaks to children in dreams. Sometimes He is showing them things about their future or revealing part of their spiritual DNA. For example, my daughter was constantly having dreams about praying for the sick, so it became apparent to me that she had the gift of healing. My son would have dreams about the church, and in order for the Lord to show the attack of the enemy, he would show the bad engines from Thomas the Train, the cartoon.

Just like the Lord will speak to our children when they are sleeping, the enemy will also try to invade their dreams with attacks. A lot of children are constantly plagued by nightmares and demonic attacks. It is important for parents to ask their children about their dreams. This will help you understand what source their dreams are coming from. When children are experiencing demonic attacks, they have to be taught how to rebuke the enemy and call on the name of Jesus. As parents, we have to pray for our children. It is so important to keep them covered and ensure the enemy does not have a foothold in their lives.

Furthermore, parents should be mindful of the doors that are opened in the lives of their children. For instance, reading books or watching television that is centered on demons and witchcraft is a method by which doors to demonic spirits are opened. Also, the same is true for toys or objects that could be considered demonic.

Many young children have been deceived by demonic spirits disguised as dead relatives or a new invisible "imaginary" friends. Once a door like this is opened, it can cause a child to be misguided by a demonic spirit that now has access to their lives.

The dream realm is just as real for children as it is for adults. As parents, we have to pay attention to the dreams of our children. What is God saying to them? What is He showing them? A lot of young children are gifted very strongly in the prophetic and will be prone to a lot of dreams and visions.

QUICK NOTE: For more information on dreams and children, I have a separate book titled, Prophetic Children: Dreams, Visions + Supernatural Encounters.

Highlights

-Children have dreams too.

-God speaks to children in a way they can understand.

- A lot of children are plagued by nightmare and demonic attacks.

- Parents have to watch out for imaginary friends.

Mental Health

/ men(t)l helTH/

    (noun) 1. a person's condition with regard to their psychological and emotional well-being.

Ref: dictionary.com

Dreams + Mental Health -12

It was stated earlier in this book that every dream is not from God nor does every dream have a spiritual advantage. We understand that some dreams can be demonic while other dreams can come from your subconscious, soul-based issues, desires, and fears, including your trauma. We also need to realize that individuals suffering from mental health related issues dream too. These dreams, for some, can feed into delusions, hopelessness, anxiety, suicidal thoughts, and hyper-religious beliefs. Individuals dealing with SMI (severe mental illness), including symptoms such as psychosis, might be unable to differentiate their dreams from actual life events.

Mental health is your emotional and psychological wellbeing. Therefore, it is so important that we recognize when dreams are from God and when they are not, because dreams can affect our mood and the way we deal with life, even when we are awake. For instance, some people are bombarded with intense dreams that cause a high level of paranoia, distress, fear, and disruption in their sleeping pattern. A lot of dreams can be very disturbing especially for people that have a lot of nightmares and dreams where they are being attacked, watched, chased or reliving a traumatic experience. Some people will have dreams where they see themselves dead or dying, or even dreams of constant failure in life. Dreams can affect our mood and be distressing, and this can affect our mental health. For some people, it seems that their dreams are directly related to their mental health diagnosis.

Scientific research has shown some possible characteristics of dreams as it relates to a person's diagnosis. [2]

Depression: Those with depression and that have suicidal thoughts/attempts have been known to have dreams about death and dying. Also, it was reported that they are prone to have dreams about misfortune and failure. The mood in their dreams are usually negative or neutral.[2]

Bi-Polar Disorder: It was stated that the dream life of those with bipolar disorder can possibly have a noticeable shift as they go from the manic phase to depressive. Many have shared how their dreams went from negative and neutral (depressive) to bizarre and unrealistic in nature (manic).[2]

Schizophrenia: People diagnosed with schizophrenia can have dreams that are relatable to their delusions while they are awake. For example, some research studies showed that some individuals diagnosed with schizophrenia had dreams primarily with strangers and a few familiar faces. Dreams were also filled with hostility directed towards them. They also tend to have a lot of nightmares. [2]

PTSD and Trauma: Studies have shown that people who have experienced extreme trauma are likely to have reoccurring dreams related to the traumatic event. Some people will have dreams that are a re-enactment of the event while others will have dreams that is relatable to the event, but not necessarily the same. [2]

A lot of people battling mental health issues are bombarded

with negative and distressing dreams; and for many, it can affect them while they are awake. Nightmares of being attacked constantly can be tormenting to someone that is paranoid when they are awake. Some individuals will intentionally stay up for days at a time to escape the torment and anguish of their dreams. Although anyone can have nightmares and disturbing dreams, it can sometimes be indicative of underlying mental health related issues.

Highlights

-A person's dreams can relate to their mental health.

-Dreams can sometimes be indicative of underlying mental health related issues.

Part 4
GOVERNING YOUR DREAMS

Governing Your Dreams -13

Govern: a to exert authority over, direct, or strongly influence the actions and conduct over something
Ref: dictionary.com

I can speak for myself when I say that I have had a lot of dreams about church leaders, nations, and global leaders. I have had dreams where I see myself having very detailed and strategic dreams with leaders of other nations. Sometimes God will show us these dreams for us to pray for certain nations and leaders. Some dreams seem to be more like an encounter. A lot of believers, especially prophets and seers, will have dreams at this magnitude. But what do you do once you have these dreams? When we see dreams about world rulers and global events, it is common to feel hopeless and think that nothing we do will have a real impact.

Does God have a purpose for these dreams? Will I meet the people that I see in my dreams? These are some of the questions that people have when they have dreams about government officials, world leaders and events on a large scale. Of course, God has a purpose for these dreams, and you might not ever meet the people you dream about in real life, but that cannot stop you from governing your dreams. Kings need the word of the Lord too, especially when their decisions can affect large groups of people.

The Bible is filled with examples of where the Lord chose to speak to powerful people over nations and many would be considered heathens. Although these heathen rulers did not serve the Lord, He still chose to speak to them in a dream.

Typically, this is because when they were at rest, that was the only way that God could get their attention. When they are asleep and having a dream, they are more prone to not dismiss what was revealed to them. The Lord is able to reveal things to men in a dream that completely shakes their inner man. They cannot soon forget what they experienced in their dreams because sometimes dreams can feel more real than life. Because God speaks to our spirit which is the real you, it explains why dreams can be so intense and feel so real because God has completely bypassed our "sleeping" flesh and is downloading directly to our spirit.

The bible shows to stand out examples of properly governing prophetic dreams. Joseph and Daniel are notable examples of how to handle dreams, specifically governmental dreams, with the wisdom of God. They both knew how to deal with leaders that were heathens but had dreams from the Lord. They both had the wisdom to give proper interpretation of what God showed in the dream. I wanted to share a few other scriptures where God was dealing with powerful leaders in the earth through dreams.

> God spoke to King Abimelech in a dream to warn him **(Genesis 20:1-8)**.
>
> Joseph interpreted Pharaoh's dream **(Genesis 41)**.
>
> King Nebuchadnezzar had dreams that troubled **him (Daniel 2)**.
>
> God appeared to King Solomon in a dream and told him to ask what he wished **(1 Kings 3:4-15)**.

Pilate's wife had a troubling dream warning them not to kill Jesus **(Matthew 27:19-23).**

GOVERN YOUR DREAMS

Taking authority

As believers, we must take authority over our dream life, including nightmares and demonic encounters. We do not have to passively allow ungodly dreams to keep happening in our lives. Sometimes, this means that we might have to repent and renounce personal and ancestral sins. A lot of believers are plagued by X-rated dreams. I have had to tell people that these dreams are not of God because these dreams are pleasurable to many people. You can rest assured in knowing that God will never show you an unclean dream. We usually open the door through sexual sin such as fornication, masturbation, and pornography. We also must ensure that we are not watching sexually charged movies and TV shows or listening to lust-driven music as it will pollute our innermost being and this can and will affect your dream life. If you listen to music and watch television that is full of lust and perversion, that will more than likely begin to spill over into your dream life. Taking authority over these types of dreams means that you are coming out of agreement with ungodly dreams.

Psalm 101:3 "I will refuse to look at anything vile and vulgar. I hate all who deal crookedly; I will have nothing to do with them."

Just like we have to actively take authority over our mind and thought life, we must do the same with our dreams. Anything that is not from God must be dismissed and rebuked. Governing our dreams is not limited to just dreams that are ungodly but this includes all dreams. There are things that we can do as believers to begin to take authority over our dream realm. In order to take authority we need discipline. We cannot govern anything without order and discipline.

Being Disciplined

To govern our dreams, we must become disciplined:

1. Immediately record your dreams so you do not forget what the Lord has spoken.
2. Find scriptures that are relevant to what God has shown you
3. Pray on a regular basis so that your spirit is strong and alert
4. Pray in the spirit on a regular basis as this builds up your spirit
5. Pray and ask God for interpretation (write down the interpretation next to the dream itself)
6. Pray and ask God how to respond to the dream once you have the interpretation
7. Live a holy life before the Lord in order to avoid tainted dreams
8. Prayer is what matures us so that we know when and if to share what the Lord has shown us.

Moving in the dream realm

If these dreams are surely from the Lord, we must respond to what He has said. Too many have gotten comfortable with having a dream, recording the dream, getting interpretation and going no further. Time to go from just dreaming and interpreting, to responding. What God has shown you in a dream many times helps to understand how to respond to that dream. Many people have the same dream over and over because they have yet to properly respond to what the Father is sharing with them.

1. **Creative dreams** [Dreams that unlock new songs, inventions, business ideas, products, books, art pieces, etc.] - After the dream is recorded, the dreamer needs to pray and begin to take the steps to create and birth into the earth what God has given them in the dream. Remaining prayerful will ensure that you are in the timing of God and doing things as HE sees fit.

2. **Governmental dreams** – These dreams can give us insight into things that we must pray against. These dreams can also give us strategy on how to pray for those that are in power in government on a local, national, or international level. There are a select few that might actually meet the people in power like Daniel or Joseph to give them wisdom and insight from the Lord. But in many cases, there is a call to depth in the place of prayer. God will sometimes show us the condition of a nation to know how to pray for the people and the leaders. Also, we will know how to help the people of the nation in a natural and practical way.

3. **Personal dreams**- I find that just like with spoken prophetic utterance, most believers do not know what

to do afterwards. Our personal dreams from God can be vital to our future. Always pray and ask for wisdom and understanding. Respond to what He has said to you and that can mean a lot of things such as;

    a. Repentance, deliverance, prayer, fasting, relocation, reconciliation, obedience, forgiving others, humility, resting in a season, going forth, sowing seeds, breaking off ungodly relationships, increasing your level of faith

4. **Dreams concerning others or groups of people** – Wisdom and prayer will let you know when, or even if, you are to share what the Lord has revealed in the dreams. Also, these dreams can in many cases be insightful and/or a call to intercede. Intercessors many times will have dreams about others, or groups of people as the Lord is giving them their prayer assignment in the form of a dream. Sometimes, the Lord will give you the interpretation of the dream and have you release a prophetic word to the person or the group of people.

Govern

/ ˈgəvərn/

(noun) 1. to exert authority over, direct, or strongly influence the actions and conduct over something.

Ref: dictionary.com

Dreams + Warfare - 14

Some of the most intense moments of warfare that I have ever experienced have been in my dreams. I cannot tell you how many times I have woke up from a dream only to feel like I was physically fighting all night long. Warfare can be intense and sometimes we will engage demonic forces while we are sleeping. When you are sleeping, your body goes through changes and adjustments such as a lowered heart rate and slowed breathing, but your spirit is always awake and does not sleep. We have to recognize that dreaming of warfare and warring against demonic powers is real. It is more than just a dream. Instead, you have encountered in the dream realm a demonic force. Many times, we need to take authority over these demonic spirits that we are engaging while we are asleep.

> **Ephesians 6:12:** "For our struggle is not against flesh and blood, but against the rulers, against the powers, against the world forces of this darkness, against the spiritual forces of wickedness in the heavenly places."

Typically, when most Spirit-filled believers think of warfare, they think of deliverance ministry, or intense time in prayer confronting demonic forces that are operating; in or against people and places. We must recognize that warfare can occur during our dreams. The spirit realm is more real than what we see. This is why many are perplexed by dreams where they feel like they are being suffocated, their breath is being snatched out of them, spirits are holding them down and they cannot move or talk.

> **Ephesians 6:11:** "Put on the whole armor of God, that you may be able to stand against the schemes of the devil."

As believers, it is vitally important to pray before we go to sleep and that we keep our spirit man built up in prayer and the word. I can remember dreaming about an internationally known religious figure, and in the dream, there was a spirit operating through him that I encountered. This was a spirit that I had never encountered before, but this demonic spirit was so strong; I was fighting with it. I literally had to call on the name of Jesus because this demon was trying to overpower me. I have had a lot of dreams where I am fighting and warring against demonic powers and forces. We must learn how to take authority and govern these types of dreams.

> **II Corinthians 10:3-5:** "For though we walk in the flesh, we are not waging war according to the flesh. For the weapons of our warfare are not of the flesh but have divine power to destroy strongholds. We destroy arguments and every lofty opinion raised against the knowledge of God, and take every thought captive to obey Christ,"

The enemy loves to beat up on people in their dreams and while they are sleeping. As we walk in our Kingdom authority, we will find that we will stop losing and gain the victory of our defeated enemy, even in our dreams. There are also benefits to dreams and warfare. Warfare dreams can also intensify the gift of discernment of spirits, as you will recognize forces that you have already encountered. As you take authority over the enemy, spirits will recognize you and the authority that you are operating with. These types of dreams can also awaken your spiritual senses. For example, the first time I smelled an unclean spirit, it was in a dream.

> **Acts 19:11-17:** "And God was doing extraordinary miracles by the hands of Paul, so that even handkerchiefs or aprons that had touched his skin were carried away to the sick, and their diseases left them and the evil spirits came out of them. Then some of the itinerant Jewish exorcists undertook to invoke the name of the Lord Jesus over those who had evil spirits, saying, "I adjure you by the Jesus whom Paul proclaims." Seven sons of a Jewish high priest named Sceva were doing this. But the evil spirit answered them, <u>"Jesus I know, and Paul I recognize, but who are you?" And the man in whom was the evil spirit leaped on them, mastered all[a] of them and overpowered them, so that they fled out of that house naked and wounded.</u> And this became known to all the residents of Ephesus, both Jews and Greeks. And fear fell upon them all, and the name of the Lord Jesus was extolled."

Warfare for some people does not end when they go to sleep. Instead, that is actually the point where it begins for many. That considered, we must learn how to navigate and handle these dreams when they are happening. When we are awake, we need to pray strategically about what we are seeing and experiencing in our dreams. We also have to ask God for clarity and understanding as to what we are warring against. One of the most common mistakes prophetic dreamers make is not asking God for clarity and more understanding. If someone is talking to you, and you don't understand what they are saying, you should always ask them to help you understand. This holds true with God as well. He doesn't want us to have dreams and not have understanding about what HE is trying to speak to us through a dream.

Warfare

/ˈwôrˌfer/

(noun) 1. Engagement in or the activities involved in war or conflict.

Ref: oxfordictionary.com

References

Dreams + Creatives

1. https://www.huffingtonpost.com/2013/11/16/famous-ideas-from-dreams_n_4276838.html

http://mentalfloss.com/article/12763/11-creative-breakthroughs-people-had-their-sleep

https://www.scienceandnonduality.com/the-secrets-of-ramanujans-garden/

https://www.famousscientists.org/7-great-examples-of-scientific-discoveries-made-in-dreams/

Dreams + Mental Health

2. https://www.psychologytoday.com/blog/dream-factory/201601/dreaming-in-depression-and-other-mental-illness